My First Animal Library

Hippopotamuses

by Penelope S. Nelson

Bullfrog Books

Ideas for Parents and Teachers

Bullfrog Books let children practice reading informational text at the earliest reading levels. Repetition, familiar words, and photo labels support early readers.

Before Reading

- Discuss the cover photo. What does it tell them?
- Look at the picture glossary together. Read and discuss the words.

Read the Book

- "Walk" through the book and look at the photos. Let the child ask questions. Point out the photo labels.
- Read the book to the child, or have him or her read independently.

After Reading

- Prompt the child to think more. Ask: Did you know about hippopotamuses before reading this book? What more would you like to learn about them after reading it?

Bullfrog Books are published by Jump!
5357 Penn Avenue South
Minneapolis, MN 55419
www.jumplibrary.com

Library of Congress Cataloging-in-Publication Data

Names: Nelson, Penelope, 1994- author.
Title: Hippopotamuses / by Penelope S. Nelson.
Description: Bullfrog books edition.
Minneapolis, MN : Jump!, Inc., [2020]
Series: My first animal library
Audience: Age 5–8. | Audience: K to Grade 3.
Includes index.
Identifiers: LCCN 2018037772 (print)
LCCN 2018039063 (ebook)
ISBN 9781641285551 (ebook)
ISBN 9781641285544 (hardcover : alk. paper)
Subjects: LCSH: Hippopotamidae—Juvenile literature.
Classification: LCC QL737.U57 (ebook)
LCC QL737.U57 N45 2019 (print)
DDC 599.63/5—dc23
LC record available at https://lccn.loc.gov/2018037772

Editor: Jenna Trnka
Designer: Jenna Casura

Photo Credits: Jesse33/Shutterstock, cover; rusm/iStock, 1; jesterpop/Shutterstock, 3; Vicki Jauron, Babylon and Beyond Photography/Getty, 4; vestica/iStock, 5; Lena Ivanova/Shutterstock, 6–7; ChuangTzuDreaming/iStock, 8–9, 23bl; JMx Images/Shutterstock, 10–11; Anton_Ivanov/Shutterstock, 12; mountainpix/Shutterstock, 13, 23br; Hansie Oosthuizen/Shutterstock, 14–15; Doug Cheeseman/Getty, 16–17, 23tl; Niels van Gijn/Getty, 18; Andrey Donnikov/iStock, 19; Goddard_Photography/iStock, 20–21, 23tr; anankkml/iStock, 22, 24.

Printed in the United States of America at Corporate Graphics in North Mankato, Minnesota.

Table of Contents

Big Swimmers

It is a hot day.

How does a hippopotamus stay cool?

It swims!

It swims underwater.

It holds its breath.

How long?

Up to 30 minutes!

Hippos even
sleep in water.

Where?

Shallow areas.

Hippos are huge!

They can be up to 14 feet (4.3 meters) long.

Wow!

On land, they are hot.

They sweat.
It is red!

Hippos go to shore at night.

They eat grass.

bloat

Many hippos
live together.

The group is
called a bloat.

Sometimes they fight.

They use their large teeth.

Wow!

Moms have one calf.
She teaches it to swim.
It will grow big!

calf

Parts of a Hippopotamus

ears
Hippo ears can fold to keep water out.

nose
Nostrils are high on the nose so they can reach above water. They can close to keep water out.

eyes
Hippo eyes are high on their head so they can peek out of water.

teeth
Hippo teeth are always growing. They can reach 20 inches (51 centimeters) in length.

legs
Hippo legs are short and thick. They help support their large bodies.

feet
Each foot has four toes. They have small webs between them to help them swim!

Picture Glossary

bloat
A group of hippopotamuses.

calf
A baby hippopotamus.

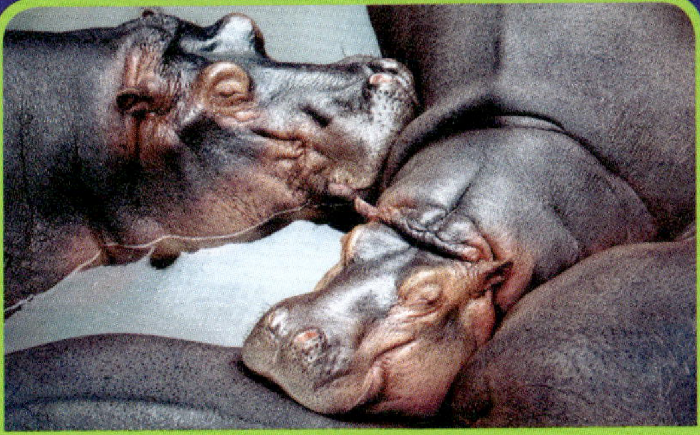

shallow
Not deep.

sweat
Moisture that comes out of the skin.

Index

To Learn More

Finding more information is as easy as 1, 2, 3.

1. Go to www.factsurfer.com
2. Enter "hippopotamuses" into the search box.
3. Click the "Surf" button to see a list of websites.